JUST THE TIP . . .

One Friday afternoon, two women are sitting on the front porch.

The first woman says, "Here comes my husband with a bunch of flowers. That means I'll be on my back with my legs in the air all weekend."

The other woman says, "Why? Don't you have a vase?"

————————

How do you make a cat drink?
Put it in a blender and extract the fur.

————————

Why don't cannibals eat clowns?
They taste funny.

————————

What's hard and hairy on the outside, soft and wet on the inside, begins with "c," ends with "t" and has the letters "u" and "n" in the middle?
A coconut.

FIENDISHLY GROSS JOKES

Volume XXXI

Julius Alvin

Zebra Books
Kensington Publishing Corp.

http://www.zebrabooks.com

ZEBRA BOOKS are published by

Kensington Publishing Corp.
850 Third Avenue
New York, NY 10022

First Printing: March 2000
10 9 8 7 6 5 4 3 2 1

Printed in the United States of America

Contents

JUST PLAIN
GROSS

Two idiots are walking down the street. They stop and one of them says, "What's that brown stuff?"

The other idiot says, "Looks like poop." He picks it up. "Feels like poop," he says. He smells it. "Smells like poop." He tastes it. "Tastes like poop."

They look at each other. "It *is* poop! Boy, am I glad we didn't step in it!"

———————

What do you call an eleven-foot-long urine stain?
Line dancing at the retirement center

———————

What is the definition of "a fart?"
A turd honking for the right of way

Why is a necrophiliac like a fur trapper?
  They're both hunting for dead beaver.

———————

What's brown and sitting on the piano bench?
  Beethoven's last movement.

———————

What's the difference between afterbirth and sand?
  You can't gargle sand.

———————

What's the difference between an oral and a rectal thermometer?
  The taste.

Edna and Bill were two residents of a nursing home who had been carrying on a love affair. They were both ninety-six years old and wheelchair bound. Every night, they would meet in the TV room. Edna would passively hold Bill's penis, and they would watch TV for an hour or so. It wasn't much, but it was all they had.

One night Bill didn't show up. He didn't show up for the next two nights either. Edna assumed he was dead, but then she saw him happily wheeling about the grounds. She confronted him and said, "Where were you these past couple of nights?"

He replied, "If you must know, I was with another woman."

"Bastard!" she cried. "What were you doing?"

"We do the exact same thing that you and I do," he answered.

"Is she prettier or younger than I am?" she asked.

"Nope. She looks the same, and she is ninety-eight years old," Bill replied.

"Well then, what does she have that I don't?" Edna asked.

Bill smiled shyly and said, "Parkinson's disease."

Harry answers the telephone, and it's an emergency room doctor. The doctor says, "Your wife was in a serious car accident, and I have bad news and good news. The bad news is she has lost all use of both arms and both legs and will need help eating and going to the bathroom for the rest of her life."

Harry says, "My God. What's the good news?"

The doctor says, "I'm kidding. She's dead."

———————

A boy in the sixth grade comes home after school one day. His mother notices that he's got a big smile on his face.

She asks, "Did anything special happen at school today?"

"Yes, Mom. I had sex with my English teacher!"

The mother is stunned. "You're going to talk about this with your father when he gets home."

Well, when dad comes home and hears the news, he is pleased as punch. Beaming with pride, he walks over to his son and says, "Son, I hear you had sex with your English teacher."

"That's right, Dad."

"Well, you became a man today. This is cause for celebration. Let's head out for some ice cream, and then I'll buy that new bike you've been asking for."

"That sounds great, Dad, but I can I have a football instead? My ass is killing me."

———————

Two men camping in the mountains had spent four days together, and they were getting a little testy. One morning, the first friend says, "You know, we're starting to get on each other's nerves. Why don't we split up today. I'll hike north and spend the day looking around. You hike south and spend the day looking around there. Then tonight, we'll have dinner and share our experiences over the campfire."

The second friend agrees and hikes south. The first man hikes north.

That night over dinner, the first man tells his story.

"Today I hiked into a beautiful valley. I followed a stream up into a canyon and ate lunch. Then I swam in a crystal-clear mountain lake. As I sat out and dried, I watched deer come and drink from the stream. The wildflowers were filled with butterflies and hawks floated all day overhead. How was your day?"

The second friend says, "I went south and ran across a set of railroad tracks. I followed them until I came across a beautiful young woman tied to the tracks. I cut the ropes off and gently lifted her off the tracks. Then we had sex in every imaginable way all afternoon. Finally, when

I was so tired I could barely move, I came back to camp.''

"Wow!'' the first guy exclaimed. "Your day was *much* better than mine. Did you get a blow job too?''

"Nah,'' says the second friend over his meal. "I couldn't find her head.''

———————

A woman complained to her doctor that she and her husband never had sex anymore. So the doctor gave her a bottle of pills and told her to put them in his drink and she would be satisfied.

The woman, somewhat disbelievingly, put one pill in his coffee that evening. That night, she and her husband made out.

The next morning, she put two pills in his coffee, and that night, they really got it on.

The next day, she said, "What the hell?'' And she put the entire bottle in. A few days later, the doctor called to check on her progress. The woman's son answered the phone. When the doctor asked how she was doing, the son replied, "Mom's dead. Sis is pregnant. My asshole hurts. And Dad is out naked on the front lawn yelling, 'Here, kitty, kitty.' ''

There were three prostitutes living together, a mother, daughter, and grandmother. One night the daughter came home, looking very down.

"How did you get on tonight, dear?" asked her mother.

"Not too good," replied the daughter. "I only got twenty dollars for a blow job."

"Wow!" said the mother. "In my day we gave a blow job for fifty cents!"

"Good God!" said the Grandmother. "In my day we were just glad to get something warm in our stomachs!"

———————

A pregnant woman walks into a bank and lines up at the first available teller. Just at that moment the bank gets robbed and she is shot three times in the stomach. She is rushed to the hospital, where she is fixed up. As she leaves, she asks the doctor about her baby.

The doctor says, "Oh! You're going to have triplets. They're fine but each one has a bullet lodged in its stomach. Don't worry though—the bullets will pass through their systems through normal metabolism."

As time goes on, the woman has three children, two girls and a boy. Twelve years later, one of the girls comes up to her mother and says, "Mommy, I've done a very weird thing!"

Her mother asks her what happened and her daughter replies, "I passed a bullet into the toilet." The woman comforts her and explains all about the accident at the bank.

A few weeks later, her other daughter comes up to her with tears streaming from her eyes. "Mommy, I've done a very bad thing!" The mother says, "Let me guess. You passed a bullet into the toilet. Right?"

The daughter looks up from her teary eyes and says, "Yes, how did you know?"

The mother comforts her child and explains the incident at the bank.

A month later the boy comes up and says, "Mommy, I've done a very bad thing!"

"You passed a bullet into the toilet. Right?"

"No, I was jerking off and shot the dog."

———————

First Patient: "I hear they brought in a case of syphilis today!"

Second Patient: "Well finally a change from Prozac."

A fellow was on his honeymoon near his favorite fishing lake. He would fish from dawn to dark with his favorite fishing guide. One day the guide, a friend of many years, mentioned that the honeymoon seemed to be spent fishing.

"Yes, but you know how I love to fish," the newlywed said.

"But aren't you newlyweds supposed to be into something else?"

"Yes, but she's got gonorrhea, and you know how I love to fish."

A few hours later, the guide says, "I understand, but that's not the only way to have sex."

"I know, but she's got diarrhea, and you know how I love to fish."

The following day, the guide says, "Sure, but that's still not the only way to have sex."

"Yeah, but she's got phyrrea, and you know how I love to fish."

Late that afternoon, thoroughly frustrated, the guide talks to the newlywed again. "I guess I'm not sure why you'd marry someone with health problems like that."

"It's 'cause she's also got worms, and you know I just love to fish."

A man goes into a greasy spoon restaurant and orders a bowl of chicken soup.

"What's this?" he screams! "There's a pussy hair in my soup! I'm not payin' for it!" And he storms out.

The waitress gets very upset at this and follows him out and sees him go to the whorehouse across the street. He pays the madam and retires to a room with a lovely blonde and goes down on her with gusto.

The waitress bursts in and says, "You complain about a hair in your soup and then come over here and do *this*?" the waitress yells.

He lifts his head, turns to her, and says, "Yeah! And if I find a noodle in here, I ain't payin' for it *either!*"

A SICK VISUAL JOKE

While you hold your palm up to your mouth and make biting gestures, say, "What's this?"

Jesus biting his nails.

A guy gets on a bus and notices a nun sitting over in a corner. Through her wimple he just spots a glimmer of her face. Gorgeous! She moves and her habit cannot hide the fact she has a truly phenomenal body. The guy gets more and more excited until he finally approaches the nun and says, "Sister, I don't normally do this sort of thing, but I think I love you. Can we get together sometime?"

The nun leaves the bus in a huff. Later as the guy is about to leave the bus himself, the bus driver asks the guy if he was the one who was bothering the nun. The guy apologizes, explaining once again that he seldom did this sort of thing, but the bus driver says, "No, don't apologize. I was checking her out myself. In fact, let me do you a favor. Did you see where she got off? There's a little park there, and every day she goes there to pray at the same time. Go there tomorrow, and maybe . . ." The guy thanks him and leaves.

Sure enough, the guy goes to the park and there's the little nun in a secluded spot by some trees. He goes off into the bushes and comes back a few minutes later with a long white robe, a long blond wig, a beard, and a crown of thorns. The nun is flabbergasted, and she asks what she can do for him. He says that every couple of thousand years, he likes to come back to earth to get laid.

The nun says that she'd love to help him, but that she had her period and would the back door be okay? He says fine, and they commence their activities. A few minutes into it, he is suddenly overcome with a blast of guilt and says, panting, "Sister, I have to tell you something. I'm not really Jesus. I'm actually the guy who was annoying you on the bus yesterday."

The nun says, "Oh, that's okay. In fact, I'm not really a nun. I'm actually the bus driver."

————————

When the Premier of India went to Moscow, the Russian President took her for a tour of the city in his limo. Recalling his visit to India, he started giving her a hard time about the sanitary conditions there.

"When I was in Delhi, I saw shit lying everywhere."

The Premier was terribly embarrassed, but only for a moment, because just ahead in Red Square was a man sitting on his heels, shitting on the side of the road. She pointed this out gleefully to the President, who was livid.

"Driver, get out immediately and shoot that man!" the President said.

The driver got out, walked up to the man with his gun drawn, spoke briefly, and then returned to the car.

"Sir, I can't shoot that man. He's the Indian ambassador."

———————

What's the difference between snot and cauliflower?

Kids will eat snot.

———————

A guy goes to prison for the first time and is put in a cell with a huge, burly guy. At lights out, the big guy gets out of his bunk and says, "We're going to have sex! You want to be the momma or the daddy?"

The very terrified new guy answers, "Uh, well, I guess I'll be the daddy."

"Okay then. Get down here and suck your momma's dick!"

A sixteen-year-old virgin girl goes to confession.

"Father, I called a man a son of a bitch yesterday."

"Why did you call him a son of bitch?" the priest asked.

"Because, Father, he touched me on my arm without permission."

"Do you mean like this?" He touches her arm.

"Yes, Father."

"That's no reason for calling him a son of a bitch."

"But, Father, he also touched my breasts."

"You mean like this?" He touches her breasts.

"Yes, Father."

"That's no reason to call him a son of a bitch."

"But, Father, he took off my clothes."

"Like this?" He takes off her clothes.

"Yes, Father."

"That's no reason to call him a son of a bitch."

"But, Father, he then put his you-know-what in my you-know-where."

"Like this?" He puts his you-know-what in her you-know-where.

"Yes, Father," she says sometime later.

"But that's no reason to call him a son of a bitch."

"But, Father, he has AIDS."

"That son of a bitch!"

When Mr. Wilkins answered the door late in the evening shortly after he'd lost his wife scuba diving, he was greeted by two grim-faced policemen.

"We're sorry to call on you at this hour, Mr. Wilkens, but we have some information about your wife."

"Well, tell me!" he demanded.

The policeman said, "We have some bad news, some pretty good news, and some really great news. Which do you want to hear first?"

Fearing the worst, Mr. Wilkins said, "Give me the bad news first."

The policeman said, "I'm sorry to tell you, sir, but we found your wife's body this morning in San Francisco Bay."

"Oh, my God!" said Mr. Wilkens, overcome by emotion. Then, remembering what the policeman had said, he asked, "What's the good news?"

"Well," said the policeman, "When we pulled her up she had two five-pound lobsters and a dozen good-size crabs on her."

"Huh?" he said, not understanding. "So what's the great news?"

The policeman smiled, licked his chops, and said, "We're going to pull her up again tomorrow morning."

WOMEN

A journalist had done a story on gender roles in Kuwait several years before the Gulf War, and she noted then that women customarily walked about 10 feet behind their husbands.

She returned to Kuwait recently and observed that the men now walked several yards behind their wives. She approached one of the women for an explanation. "This is marvelous," said the journalist. "What enabled women here to achieve this reversal of roles?"

Replied the Kuwaiti woman, "Land mines."

———————

A woman with really hairy armpits got on a crowded bus. Unable to find a seat, she settled on hanging on to one of the poles.

A drunk man next to her stared at her for three minutes, then said, "I love a woman who does aerobics."

The woman replied angrily, "I don't *do* aerobics!"

The drunk man then looked at the woman and said, "Then how did you get your leg up so high?"

———————

Two guys are sitting in a bar. One turns to the other and says, "Did you know that in this country alone there are over a half million battered women?"

"No shit," the other guy says. "All this time I've been eating them plain."

———————

Why don't blondes' intestines fall out of their cunts?

The vacuums in their heads hold them in.

———————

What's the difference between an epileptic oyster shucker and a prostitute with diarrhea?

One shucks between fits.

A girl goes into a bar, pulls up a stool and says, "Bartender, give me a triple Jack Daniel's."

He gives her a triple Jack Daniel's, and she belts it down. She has five more in a row, belts them all down, passes out dead drunk, and everybody in the bar fucks her.

The next night, she walks into the bar, and says, "Bartender, give me a triple Jack Daniel's."

He gives her a triple Jack Daniel's, and she belts it down. She has five more in a row, belts them all down, passes out dead drunk, and everybody in the bar fucks her again.

The next night, she walks into the bar and says, "Bartender, give me a triple Tequila."

"I thought you drank Jack Daniel's."

"Not anymore. Jack Daniel's makes my pussy sore."

Hillary Clinton gets on *Password* as the celebrity contestant. It's her turn to guess the secret word, which is "black dick."

Hillary: Um . . . is it a place?

Her partner: No.

Hillary: Is it a person?

Her partner: No.

Hillary: Hmm, then it must be a thing. Um, is it something I might want to eat?

Her partner, exasperated: Well, I dunno, maybe.

Hillary: Is it "black dick?"

_____

Gynecologist: You have acute vaginitis.

Blonde: Thank you.

_____

Two young lovers go up to the mountains for a romantic winter vacation. When they get there, the guy goes out to chop some wood. When he gets back, he says, "Honey, my hands are freezing!"

She says, "Well, put them here between my thighs and that will warm them up."

After lunch, he goes back out to chop some more wood and comes back and says again, "Man! My hands are really freezing!"

She says again, "Well, put them here between my thighs and warm them up." He does, and again that warms him up.

After dinner, he goes out one more time to chop some wood to get them through the night. When he returns, he says again, "Honey, my hands are really, really freezing!"

She looks at him and says, "For crying out loud, don't your ears ever get cold?"

THE TEN MOST IMPORTANT PEOPLE IN A WOMAN'S LIFE

1. The doctor because he says, "Take off your clothes."

2. The dentist because he says, "Open wide."

3. The hairdresser because he says, "Do you want it teased or blown?"

4. The milkman because he says, "Do you want it in front or in back?"

5. The interior decorator because he says, "Once you have it all in, you'll love it."

6. The banker because he says, "If you take it out to soon, you'll lose interest."

7. The police officer because he says, "Spread 'em"

8. The mailman because he always delivers his package.

9. The pilot because he takes off fast and then slows down.

10. The hunter because he always goes deep in the bush, shoots twice, and eats what he shoots.

————————

What did Joan Collins say to King Kong?
  Is it in yet?

————————

What's the difference between a whore and a bitch?
  A whore screws everyone. A bitch screws everyone except you.

————————

How do girls get minks?
  The same way minks get minks.

Why don't women have any brains?

Because they don't have penises to keep them in.

———————

Why don't men trust women?

Would you trust anything that bled for three days and didn't die?

———————

What do you call a fat woman with a yeast infection?

A Whopper with cheese.

GROSS
CELEBRITY
JOKES

What's the difference between Princess Diana and Tiger Woods?
  Tiger has a better driver.

_____

What does DIANA stand for?
  Died In A Nasty Accident.

_____

Did you hear that Di has something in common with George Burns?
  They both died when they hit a hundred.

Did you hear about the princess who stayed out after midnight?

She turned into a pillar of concrete.

———————

Did you hear Pizza Hut is announcing a "Princess Di Meatlover's Pizza?"

It's made with two kinds of meat: Egyptian sausage and Welsh beaver.

———————

What is the difference between a Mercedes and a Skoda?

Princess Diana wouldn't be seen dead in a Skoda.

———————

What were Di's last words to her lover?

"Take me up the tunnel and make me scream."

When is Diana, Princess of Wales, not Diana, Princess of Wales?
  When she's Di-in-a car crash!

Why was the pillar red?
  Because it had Di on it.

Did you hear about Diana on the radio?
  . . . on the dashboard?
  . . . on the steering wheel?

Why was Diana so thin?
  Because she was on a crash diet.

Heard about the new film?
  Crash 2: The Royal Sequel.

Why did Diana die?

So she could be the first person in the Versace '98 collection.

———————

What is Diana's favorite band?

Crash Test Dummies.

———————

What is the queen giving Fergie for Christmas?

A black Mercedes and a trip to Paris.

———————

What is the difference between Michael Jackson and a grocery bag?

One is made of plastic and is dangerous for children to play with. The other is used to carry groceries.

What did Jeffrey Dahmer say to Pee Wee Herman in their holding cell at the jail?
  "Stop playing with my lunch."

_____

Why does Mike Tyson cry during sex?
  Mace.

_____

What is the difference between Prince Charles and O.J. Simpson?
  Prince Charles's ex-wife was killed by a white man in a black car.

_____

What is blonde, has six legs, and roams Michael Jackson's dreams every night?
  Hanson.

How do you satisfy Bill Clinton's sexual appetite?
  It takes a village.

_____

What does Hillary Clinton do right after she shaves her pussy?
  She sends him to work.

_____

What's brown and often found in children's underpants?
  Michael Jackson's hand.

_____

What's the difference between Courtney Love and Wayne Gretzky?
  Wayne takes a shower after three periods.

What's the difference between Michael Jackson and greyhound racing?

The greyhounds wait for the hares to come out.

What's foreplay in Arkansas?

When Bill says, "Brace yourself, Hillary."

What was the last thing to go through Princess Di's head?

The radiator.

What was the fabric of Princess Di's dress?

Crushed velvet.

Why did Elton John sing at Diana's funeral?
    Because he's the only queen who gives a fuck.

———————

Why couldn't Marv Albert's girlfriend become a sportscaster too?
    NBC gave her an audition but she sucked.

———————

What do you call five dogs with no balls?
    The Spice Girls!

———————

What do Chris Farley, Michael Kennedy, and Sonny Bono have in common?
    They all died on white powder.

What do you call a thousand heavily armed lesbians?

Militia Etheridge.

What does "Bones" McCoy say before he performs brain surgery on a blonde?

"Space. The final frontier."

TOTAL
GROSS-OUTS

How do you know that a female bartender is pissed off at you?

There's a little white thread hanging out of your Bloody Mary.

———————

What sucks blood and has wings?

A maxi-pad.

———————

What's grosser than gross?

Two vampires fighting over a bloody tampon.

What is a man's idea of protected sex?
    A padded headboard.

_____

What do you call a thousand-pound lady with a condom in her pocket?
    A half ton with a box liner.

_____

Two condoms are walking down the street when, upon passing by a gay bar, one turns to the other and says, "Hey—wanna' go in and get shit faced?"

_____

Two kindergarten girls were talking outside.
    One said, "You won't believe what I saw on the patio yesterday—a condom!"
    The second girl asked, "What's a patio?"

This guy walks into the bathroom of the bar and sees this other guy standing in front of the condom machine chewing furiously with this really pissed off look on his face.

"What's the matter, buddy?" he asks.

"This gum really sucks," the guy says.

"Yeah, I know," says the first guy as he sticks a quarter in the machine, "but it lasts a long time and sure as hell makes big bubbles."

SILLY SLOGANS FOR NATIONAL CONDOM WEEK

Cover Your Stump Before You Hump.
Before You Attack Her . . . Wrap Your Wacker.
Don't Be Silly . . . Protect Your Willie.
Before You Blast Her, Guard Your Bushmaster.
Don't Be A Loner . . . Cover Your Boner.
When In Doubt, Shroud Your Spout.
You Can't Go Wrong If You Shield Your Dong.
It You're Not Going To Sack It, Go Home And Wack It.
If You Think She's Spunky, Cover Your Monkey.
Before You Bag Her, Sheath Your Dagger.
It'll Be Sweeter If You Wrap Your Peter.
If You Slip Between Thighs, Be Sure You Condomize.

To Save Embarrassment Later, Cover Your 'Gator.'

She Won't Get Sick If You Cap Your Dick.

If You Go Into Heat, Package Your Meat.

While You're Undressing Venus, Dress Up That Penis.

When You Take Off Her Pants 'N Blouse, Suit Up That Trouser Mouse.

Don't Do More Than Neck Her With An Unwrapped Pecker.

Especially In December, Gift Wrap Your Member.

Befo' Da Van Start Rockin', Be Sho' Yo' Cock Gots A Stockin'.

Don't Be A Fool, Vulcanize Your Tool.

The Right Selection, Sack That Erection.

Wrap It In Foil Before Checking Her Oil.

A Crank With Armor Will Never Harm Her.

Don't Be In A Jiffy . . . Cover Your Stiffy.

———————

How is a woman like a condom?
   If she's not on your dick, she's in your wallet.

———————

What do Kodak and a condom have in common?
   You use both to catch those special moments!

What does the serial number on a condom look like?

Give up? Well, I guess you never had to unroll one that far. . . .

———————

Why won't tampons speak to you on the street?

They're stuck up cunts.

———————

A young man goes into a drug store to buy condoms. The pharmacist says the condoms come in packs of three, nine or twelve and asks which the young man wants.

"Well," he said, "I've been seeing this girl for a while and she's really hot. I want the condoms because I think tonight's *the* night. We're having dinner with her parents, and then we're going out. And I've got a feeling I'm gonna get lucky after that. Once she's had me, she'll want me all the time. So you'd better give me the twelve pack."

The young man makes his purchase and leaves.

Later that evening, he sits down to dinner with his girlfriend and her parents. He asks if he might give the blessing, and they agree. He begins the prayer, but continues praying for several minutes.

The girl leans over and says, "You never told me that you were such a religious person."

He leans over to her and says, "You never told me that your father is a pharmacist."

———————

Sign on the door of a gay bar: *Condoms Fitted Free.*

———————

What's the difference between a blimp and a thousand used condoms?

One's a Goodyear. The other's a damn good year!

What do you call a used tampon floating in a river?

A blood vessel.

_____

Why do women stop bleeding when entering menopause?

Because they need all the blood for their varicose veins!

_____

One day, two vampires walked into a pretty scary bar. The first one said, "May I please have a glass of warm blood?"

"Certainly," replied the barman. "And what would you like?"

"A glass of warm water please," said the second vampire.

A few minutes later, the barman returned with a glass of blood and a glass of warm water. The barman says, "You're a vampire, aren't you? Surely you drink blood."

The second vampire pulls out a tampon and tells him, "I brought a tea bag."

GROSS
HARD-NOSED
GUY JOKES

Two guys were hunting and got separated. Joe decided to take a dump, and after hanging his ass over a log, he soon fell asleep. Meanwhile, his buddy shot a deer. While dragging it back to his rig, he noticed his buddy asleep on the log. As a prank, he gutted the deer and placed the pile of guts under his friend's ass. After returning to the truck, he too was tired and took a nap.

A couple hours later, he awoke to see Joe trundling across the field. "What the hell's wrong with you, Joe? Looks like you seen a ghost!"

"Well, I hung my ass over a log to take a dump, and while I was a sleep, I must have shit my guts out. It if wasn't for the grace of God and a greasy stick I would never have gotten 'em back in."

A guy walks into a Wells Fargo bank and says to the teller, "Hey, bitch! I wanna open a fuckin' account!"

"Excuse me?"

"I said I wanna open a fuckin account!"

"Sir, that language is intolerable!" she exclaimed. "I'm getting a manager!"

The manager comes along and asks, "Sir, is there a problem?"

"No," he replies, "I just wanna open a fuckin' account!"

The manager says, "Sir, we do not use that kind of language at this bank."

The man says, "Listen. I just won thirty-five million dollars in the goddamn lottery and I wanna open a fuckin' account!"

The manager points to the teller and responds, "And this bitch is giving you a hard time?"

———————

There's a guy hitchhiking along the highway when along comes an eighteen-wheeler. It pulls up and comes to a grinding halt. The hitcher runs to the truck, reaches up, opens the door, and jumps in. Inside the truck is the driver, and beside him is his pet monkey.

"Great-lookin' monkey, buddy," said the hitcher.

"Yeah, he's great company, and he looks after you as well. Take a look at this."

Without further ado, the trucker winds up and punches the monkey in the guts with all his might. The monkey dutifully bends down, unzips the trucker's fly, goes down, and starts to flow the truck driver. Once the trucker has unloaded his cargo all over the cabin, the monkey wipes him off, zips up his fly, and sits back down in his seat in the cabin.

"That's great!" says the hitchhiker. "Can I try it?"

The driver looks across and replies, "Yeah, sure. Why not?"

"There's only one thing though," says the hitcher.

"What?"

"There's no need to smack me in the guts so hard."

A lawyer from New York was transferred to a small frontier town during the settlement of the West. After several weeks there he noticed that the town was populated solely by men.

He asked one of the local cowboys, "What do you do when you get the urge for a woman?"

The cowboy replied, "See them thar sheep up on thet hill. We just go git us one."

"That is disgusting and barbaric!" replied the lawyer.

After about three months the lawyer could not stand it any longer. He decided though, if he was going to do a sheep, he would show these yokels how to do it right. He picked out the prettiest sheep of the bunch, bathed her, put a pink ribbon on her, served her hay on a china plate, dressed her in fine lingerie, and then took the sheep to bed.

After he finished he decided to take his new-found lover out for a drink. He wandered into the local saloon with the sheep under his arm. The piano fell silent, people dropped drinks, and all the cowboys turned and stared in shocked disbelief.

The lawyer said, "You bunch of hypocrites. You look at me as if I'm some sort of freak for doing what you've been doing all along. I'm just doing it with more class."

"That ain't the problem," replied one cowboy. "That's the sheriff's gal you're with."

———————

Sam quits his pressure-job and buys fifty acres of land in Vermont as far from humanity as possible. Sam sees the postman once a week and gets groceries once a month. Otherwise it's total peace and quiet. After six months or so of almost total isolation, he's finishing dinner when someone knocks on his door. He opens it and there is a big, bearded Vermonter standing there.

"Name's Enoch—your neighbor from four miles over the ridge. Having a party Saturday. Thought you'd like to come."

"Great," says Sam, "after six months of this, I'm ready to meet some local folks. Thank you."

As Enoch is leaving, he stops, "Gotta warn you there's gonna be some drinkin'."

"Not a problem. After twenty-five years in business, I can drink with the best of 'em."

Again, as Enoch starts to leave, he stops. "More 'n likely gonna be some fightin' too."

Damn, Sam thinks, *tough crowd*. "Well, I get along with people. I'll be there. Thanks again."

Once again, Enoch turns from the door. "I've seen some wild sex at these parties too."

"Now that's not a problem," says Sam. "Remember I've been alone for six months! I'll definitely be there. By the way, what should I wear?"

Enoch stops in the door again and says, "Whatever you want. Just gonna be the two of us."

———————

One day after striking gold in Alaska, a lonesome miner came down from the mountains and walked into a saloon in the nearest town.

"I'm lookin' for the meanest, roughest, toughest whore in the Yukon!" he said to the bartender.

"We got her!" replied the barkeep. "She's upstairs in the second room on the right."

The miner handed the bartender a gold nugget to pay for the whore and two beers. He grabbed the bottles, stomped up the stairs, kicked open the second door on the right, and yelled, "I'm lookin' for the meanest, roughest, toughest whore in the Yukon!"

The woman inside the room looked at the miner and said, "You found her!"

Then she stripped naked, bent over, and grabbed her ankles.

"How do you know I want to do it in that position?" asked the miner.

"I don't," replied the whore. "I just thought you might like to open those beers first."

A guy walks into an elevator and stands next to a beautiful woman. After a few minutes he turns to her and says, "Can I smell your pussy?"

The woman looks at him in disgust and says, "Certainly not!"

"Hmmm," he replies. "It must be your feet then."

A man was walking along the street when he saw a ladder going into the clouds. As any of us would do, he climbed the ladder. He reached a cloud, upon which sat a rather plump and very ugly woman. "Screw me or climb the ladder to success," she said.

No contest, thought the man. So he climbed the ladder to the next cloud. On this cloud was a slightly thinner woman, slightly easier on the eye.

"Screw me hard or climb the ladder to success," she said.

Well, thought the man, *might as well carry on.*

On the next cloud was an even more attractive lady, who, this time, was actually quite desirable. "Screw me now or climb the ladder to success," she said. As he turned her down and went on up the ladder, the man thought to himself that this was getting better the further he went.

On the next cloud was an absolute beauty. Slim, attractive, the lot.

"Love me hard and long or climb the ladder to success," she flirted.

Unable to imagine what could be waiting and being a gambling man, he decided to climb again.

When he reached the next cloud, there was a fat, ugly man with armpit hair showing, and flies buzzing around his head.

"Who are you?" the man who'd climbed the ladder asked.

"Hello," the ugly fat man said. "My name's Cess!"

Three guys are discussing women.

"I like to watch a woman's tits best," the first guy says.

The second says, "I like to look at a woman's ass." He asks the third guy, "What about you?"

"Me? I prefer to see the top of her head."

———————

Why do women take longer than men to reach orgasm?

Who cares?

———————

How do you know when it's time to wash dishes and clean the house?

Look inside your pants. If you have a penis, it's not time.

———————

A black guy and a gorilla go into a bar together. The black guy says to the bartender, "I'd like a beer and a gin and tonic for my girlfriend here."

The bartender says, "Oh, come on, pal. We don't serve no gorillas in here."

So the guy figures he'll fix them. He takes the gorilla home, shaves off all her hair, gives her a nice wig, lipstick, red dress, etc. He takes her back to the bar and says, "I'd like a beer and a gin and tonic for my girlfriend here."

The bartender gives them the drinks and they go off and sit down and chat. The bartender turns to his buddy at the bar and says, "You know, that drives me crazy. It seems like every time a good-looking Italian girl comes in here, she's with a black guy."

———————

A Jewish man, a Roman Catholic man, and a Morman man were chatting one day and the subject of family size came up. The Jewish man said, "My wife just gave birth. Now I have enough to fill out a basketball team."

The Roman Catholic responded, "With the recent addition to our family, I now have enough to fill out a baseball team!"

To which the Morman man retorted, "When I marry my next wife I'll have enough to stock a country club."

A bunch of guys are hanging around the bar telling Polish jokes. One thing leads to another and things get pretty wild. Pretty soon this big guy walks over and says, "Hey, assholes. I'm Polish and I don't like you telling all those Polish jokes!"

One of the guys says, "Well, they're not against you, pal, just anyone who lives in Poland."

"My mother's in Poland!" he screams and pulls out a razor.

Just in time his friends pull him back to his table and things quiet down. A little later one of his friends walks over to the subdued crowd of guys.

"You don't know how lucky you assholes are," he says.

"Oh, yeah," says one of the guys. "Why?"

"If he could've found a place to plug it in, he would have killed you."

Two guys in a bar are passing the time talking about fucking.

"Do you know what a *rodeo fuck* is?" the first guy says.

"Never heard of it," says his friend.

"Goes like this: Your babe gets on all fours. You mount up, making sure you have a good grip. Then you say, "Honey, you're the worst piece of ass I ever had!"

"What's the big deal about that?" asks the friend.

"You think it's easy? You try to hold on for eight seconds."

––––––––––––

John receives a phone call. "Hello," he answers.

The voice on the other end says, "This is Susan. We met at a party about three months ago."

John: "Hmm . . . Susan? About three months ago?"

Susan: "Yes, it was at Bill's house. After the party you took me home. On the way we parked and got into the backseat. You told me I was a good sport."

John: "Oh, yeah! Susan! How are you?"

Susan: "I'm pregnant and I'm going to kill myself."

John: "Say, you *are* a good sport."

Two men are approaching each other on a sidewalk. Both are dragging their right foot as they walk. As they meet, one man looks at the other knowingly, points at his foot and says, "Vietman, 1969."

The other hooks his thumb behind him says, "Dog shit, twenty feet back."

TRULY GROSS
FAMILY JOKES

The composition teacher asked the class to write about an unusual event that happened during the past week. Little Johnny got up and read his essay. He began, "Daddy fell into the well last week . . ."

"My goodness!" the teacher exclaimed. "Is he all right?"

"He must be," said the boy. "He stopped yelling for help yesterday."

———

Billy Joe and Betty Sue get married, and Billy Joe whisks her away to his daddy's hunting cabin in the woods for a romantic nature honeymoon. He carries her across the threshold, and they get into bed. Then Betty Sue whispers in his ear, "Billy Joe, be gentle, I ain't never been with a man b'fore."

"What?" shouts Billy Joe, and his little bride

softly shakes her head. Billy Joe jumps out of bed, grabs his clothes, and races out the door and into his truck. Then he drives down the mountain, straight to his parents house. He rushes inside screaming "Hey, Daddy! Git up!"

His father rushes downstairs and gasps, "Billy Joe, what'r you doin here?"

Billy Joe, still breathing hard from his mad flight, gasps, "Well, Betty Sue an' I was in the cabin, an' she told me she ain't never been with a man afore. So I rushed outta there an' lit back here quick as I could!"

His father grasps Billy Joe's shoulder in reassurance and says, "Son, ya done the right thing. If'n she ain't good 'nuff fer her family, she shure as shit ain't good 'nuff fer ours!"

———————

One evening a man was at home watching TV and eating peanuts. He'd toss them in the air, then catch them in his mouth. In the middle of catching one, his wife asked a question, and as he turned to answer her, a peanut fell in his ear. He tried and tried to dig it out, but succeeded in only pushing it in deeper. He called his wife for assistance, and after hours of trying, they became worried and decided to go to the hospital.

As they were ready to go out the door, their

daughter came home with her date. After being informed of the problem, their daughter's date said he could get the peanut out. The young man told the father to sit down, then shoved two fingers up the father's nose and told him to blow hard. When the father blew, the peanut flew out. The mother and daughter jumped and yelled for joy. The young man insisted it was nothing, and the daughter brought the young man out to the kitchen for something to eat. Once he was gone the mother turned to the father.

The mother said, "That's wonderful. Isn't he smart? What do you think he's going to be when he grows older?"

The father replies, "From the smell of his fingers, our son-in-law!"

———————

A guy works a new job on Thursday and Friday. On Monday he calls in and says, "I can't come in today. I'm sick." He works the rest of the week, but the following Monday he calls in and says, "I can't come in today. I'm sick."

The boss asks the foreman about him, and the foreman says, "He's great. He does the work of two men. We need him."

So the boss calls the guy into his office and says, "You seem to have a problem getting to work on Mondays. You're a good worker and I'd hate to fire you. What's the problem? Anything we can help you with? Drugs? Alcohol?"

The guy says, "No, I don't drink or do drugs. But my brother-in-law drinks every weekend and then beats on my sister. So every Monday morning, I go over to make sure she's all right. She puts her head on my shoulder and cries. One thing leads to another, and the next thing you know, I'm fucking her."

The boss says, "You fuck your sister?"

The guy says, "Hey, I told you I was sick."

———————

This little boy and his grandfather are fishing. Granddad pulls out a beer and the little boy says "Grandpa, can I have one of those?"

Grandpa says, "Is your penis big enough to touch your asshole?"

"No," the little boy responds.

"Then you can't have one."

A while later, the granddad pulls out a cigar and the boy asks, "Can I have one of those?"

Grandpa says, "Is your penis big enough to touch your asshole?"

"No," the little boy responds.

"Then you can't have one."

Later on, grandpa and grandson go to the grocery store for food and each buys a lottery ticket. Grandpa is unlucky, but the little boy says, "I just won fifty grand."

Grandpa says, "Great. You're going to split that with me. Right?"

The little boy asks, "Grandpa, is your penis long enough to touch your asshole?"

"Yes," says grandpa.

"Then go fuck yourself."

———————

One Sunday morning Joe burst into the living room and said, "Dad, Mom, I have some great news for you! I am getting married to the most beautiful girl in town. She lives a block away and her name is Susan."

After dinner, Joe's dad took him aside, "Son, I have to talk to you. Your mother and I have been married thirty years. She's a wonderful wife, but she has never offered much excitement in the bedroom. So I used to fool around with women a lot. Susan is actually your half sister, and I'm afraid you can't marry her."

Joe was heartbroken. After eight months he eventually started dating girls again. A year later he came home and very proudly announced, "Diane said yes! We are getting married in June."

Again his father insisted on another private conversation and broke the sad news. "Diane is your half sister too, Joe. I am very sorry about this."

Joe was furious! He finally decided to go to his mother with the news.

"Dad has done so much harm. I guess I am never going to get married," he complained. "Every time I fall in love, Dad tells me the girl is my half sister."

His mother just shook her head. "Don't pay any attention to what he says, dear. He's not really your father."

———————

This butcher lived in an apartment over his shop. One night he was awakened by strange noises coming from below, so he tiptoed downstairs and saw his nineteen-year-old daughter sitting on the chopping block and masturbating with a liverwurst. The butcher sighed and tiptoed back to bed.

The next morning, when a customer walked in and asked for some liverwurst, the butcher said that he didn't have any left. The customer was really annoyed. She pointed to the corner of the shop and asked, "No liverwurst? Well, what's that hanging on the hook right over there?"

The butcher frowned at her. "That," he replied, "is my son-in-law."

One fall day, Bill was out raking leaves when he noticed a hearse slowly drive by. Following the first hearse was a second hearse, which was followed by a man walking solemnly along, followed by a dog, and then about two hundred men walking in single file.

Intrigued, Bill went up to the man following the second hearse and asked him who was in the first hearse.

"My wife," the man replied.

"I'm sorry," said Bill. "What happened to her?"

"My dog bit her and she died."

Bill then asked the man who was in the second hearse.

The man replied, "My mother-in-law. My dog bit her and she died as well."

Bill thought about this for a while. He finally asked the man, "Can I borrow your dog?"

To which the man replied, "Get in line."

At the 1997 World Women's Conference a speaker from England stood up. "At last year's conference we spoke about being more assertive with our husbands. Well after the conference I went home and told my husband that I would no longer cook for him and that he would have to do it himself. After the first day I saw nothing. After the second day I saw nothing. But after the third day I saw that he had cooked a wonderful roast lamb."

The crowd cheered.

Then a speaker from America stood up. "After last year's conference I went home and told my husband that I would no longer do his laundry and that he would have to do it himself. After the first day I saw nothing. After the second day I saw nothing. But after the third day I saw that he had done not only his own washing but my washing as well."

The crowd cheered.

Then a speaker from Australia stood up. "After last year's conference I went home and told my husband that I would no longer do his shopping and that he would have to do it himself. After the first day I saw nothing. After the second day I saw nothing. But after the third day I could see a little bit out of my left eye."

———————

A little kid comes running into the backyard. He says, "Pop! Pop! Ma just got hit by a bus!"

"Son, you know my lips are chapped. Please don't make me smile."

An escaped convict broke into a house and tied up a young couple who had been sleeping in the bedroom.

As soon as he had a chance, the husband turned to his voluptuous young wife, bound up on the bed in a skimpy nightgown, and whispered, "Honey, this guy hasn't seen a woman in years. Just do anything he wants. If he wants to have sex with you, just go along with it and pretend you like it. Our lives depend on it."

"Dear," the wife hissed, spitting out her gag, "I'm so relieved you feel that way, because he just told me he thinks you have a really nice, tight-looking ass!"

———————

A guy goes over to his friend's house, rings the bell, and the wife answers.

"Hi, is Tony home?"

"No, he went to the store."

"Well, you mind if I wait?"

"No, come in."

They sit down and the friend says, "You know, Nora, you have the greatest breasts I have ever seen. I'd give you a hundred bucks if I could just see one naked."

Nora thinks about this for a second and figures it'd be worth it for a hundred bucks. She opens her robe and shows one breast. He promptly thanks her and throws a hundred bucks on the table.

They sit there a while longer and Chris says, "They are so beautiful I've got to see the both of them. I'll give you another hundred bucks if I could just see the both of them together."

Nora thinks about this, then opens her robe and gives Chris a nice long look. Chris thanks her, throws another hundred bucks on the table, and then says he can't wait any longer and leaves.

A while later Tony arrives home and his wife says, "You know, your weird friend Chris came over."

Tony thinks about this for a second and says, "Well, did he drop off the two hundred bucks he owes me?"

Three guys are applying for a job with the CIA. They get all the way to the final test.

So the first guy walks into the director's office and sits down. The director reaches in his desk and pulls out a pistol. He lays it on his desk in front of the guy and tells him, "This is a test of your loyalty. Take this gun and go up the stairs and go into the first room on your right. Your wife will be in there. Put a bullet in her head."

The guy looks at him and says, "No way."

So the director says, "You fail."

The next guy comes in. The director tells him

the same thing. The guy picks up the gun and heads for the room. He comes back about fifteen minutes later. He tells the director that he just couldn't go through with it.

The director says, "You fail."

So now the third guy comes in. Same scene. The guy heads up to the room. The director hears three shots, followed by a whole lot of ruckus. The guy comes back in all beat up with his clothes torn up.

The director says, "What happened to you?"

The guy replies, "After three shots I realized that there were blanks in the gun, so I had to choke the bitch to death."

———————

A woman accomanied her husband to the doctor's office. After the checkup, the doctor took the wife aside and said, "Your husband is suffering from severe, long-term stress and it's affecting his cardiovascular system. He's a good candidate for either a heart attack or a stroke. If you don't do the following four things, your husband will surely die.

"First, each morning, fix him a healthy breakfast and send him off to work in a good mood.

"Second, at lunch time, make him a warm, nutritious meal and put him in a good frame of mind before he goes back to work.

"Third, for dinner, fix an especially nice meal, and don't burden him with household chores.

"Fourth, and most important for invigorating him and relieving stress, have sex with him several times a week and satisfy his every whim in bed."

On the way home in the car, the husband turned to his wife and asked, "So I saw the doctor talking to you and he sure seemed serious. What did he tell you?"

"You're going to die," she replied.

A husband and wife were having difficulty surviving financially, so they decided that the wife should try prostitution as an extra source of income. The husband drove her out to a popular corner and informed her he would be at the side of the building if she had any questions or problems.

A gentleman pulled up shortly after and asked her how much she wanted to go all the way. She told him to wait a minute and ran around the corner to ask her husband. The husband told her to tell the client a hundred bucks. She went back and informed the client, and he cried, "That's too much!"

He then asked, "How much for a hand job?" She asked him to wait a minute and ran to ask her husband how much. The husband said to ask for forty bucks. The woman ran back and informed the client. He felt that this was an agreeable price and began to remove his pants and underwear. Upon the removal of his clothing the woman noticed that the man was really well hung.

She asked him once more to wait a moment. She ran around the corner again and her husband asked, "Now what?"

The wife replied, "Can I borrow sixty bucks?"

———————

Father, mother, and son decided to go to the zoo one day. So they set off and are seeing lots of animals. Eventually they end up opposite the elephant house. The boy looks at the elephant, sees its dick, points to it, and says, "Mummy, what is that long thing?"

His mother replies, "That, son, is the elephant's trunk."

"No, at the other end."

"That, son, is the tail."

"No, Mummy, the thing under the elephant."

After a short embarrassed silence she replies, "That's nothing."

The mother goes to buy some ice cream and the boy, not being satisfied with her answer, asks his father the same question.

"Daddy, what is that long thing?"

"That's the trunk, son," replies the father.

"No at the other end."

"Oh, that is the tail."

"No, no, Daddy, the thing below," asks the son in desperation.

"That is the elephant's penis. Why do you ask, son?"

"Well, Mummy said it was nothing," says the boy.

Replies the father, "I tell you, son, I spoil that woman."

———————

A man comes home from work and finds his wife admiring her breasts in the mirror. He asks, "What are you doing?"

She replies, "I went to the doctor today, and he told me I have the breasts of a twenty-five year old."

The husband retorts, "Well, what did he say about your fifty-year-old ass?"

She replies, "Frankly, dear, your name never came up."

It's a beautiful spring day and a man and his wife are at the zoo. She's wearing a cute, loose-fitting, pink dress. As they walk through the ape exhibit and pass in front of a very large gorilla, the gorilla goes wild. He jumps up on the bars, holding on with one hand, grunting and pounding his chest with the free hand. He is obviously excited about the pretty lady in the wavy dress. The husband, noticing the excitement, suggests that his wife tease the poor fellow.

The husband suggests she pucker her lips, wiggle her bottom, and play along. She does and the gorilla gets even more excited, making noises that would wake the dead. Then the husband suggests that she let one of her straps fall. She does, and the gorilla is just about to tear the bars down.

"Now try lifting your dress up your thighs."

This drives the gorilla absolutely crazy.

Then, the husband quickly grabs his wife by the hair, rips open the door to the cage, flings her in with the gorilla, and says, "Now, tell *him* you have a headache."

———————

A man came home from work sporting two black eyes.

"What happened to you?" asked his wife.

"I'll never understand women," he replied.

"I was riding up an escalator behind this pretty young girl, and I noticed that her skirt was stuck in the crack of her ass. So I pulled it out, and she turned around and punched me in the eye!"

"I can certainly appreciate that," said the wife. "But how did you get the second black eye?"

"Well, I figured she liked it that way," said the husband. "So I pushed it back in."

———————

A young couple are on their way to Vegas to get married. Before getting there, the girl says to the guy that she has a confession to make. The reason that they have not been too intimate is because she is very flat chested. If he wishes to cancel the wedding, it's okay with her. The guy thinks for a while and says he does not mind she is flat because sex is not the most important thing in a marriage.

Several miles down the road, the guy turns to the girl and says that he also wants to make a confession. He says below his waist he is just like a baby. If the girl wants to cancel the marriage, it's okay with him. The girl thinks for a while and says that she does not mind. She also believes there are other things far more important than sex in a marriage.

They are happy that they are honest with each

other. They go on to Vegas and get married. On their wedding night, the girl takes off her clothes. She is as flat as a washboard. Finally, the guy takes off his clothes. One glance at the guy's naked body, and the girl faints and falls to the floor.

After she comes to, the guy says, "I told you before we got married. Why did you still faint?"

The girl says "You told me it was just like a baby."

The guy replies, "Yes, eight pounds and twenty-one inches."

A man has six children and he is very proud of his achievement. He is so proud of himself that he starts calling his wife "Mother of Six" in spite of her objections.

One night they go to a party. The man decides that it's time to go home, and he wants to find out if his wife is ready to leave as well. He shouts at the top of his voice, "Shall we go home, Mother of Six?"

His wife, irritated by her husband's lack of discretion, shouts back, "Anytime you're ready, Father of Four!"

This guy is sitting in his living room, surfing the channels on the television. All of a sudden, the door of the apartment whips open and his girlfriend storms through.

She screams, "You fucking asshole!" and she heads into the bedroom.

Stunned, the man flips off the television and walks toward the bedroom, wondering, *Now what have I done?*

Inside the bedroom he finds the girl furiously packing a suitcase. He asks her what's up. She responds with a hiss, "My therapist says that I should leave you and that you're a pedophile!"

The man responds, "Wow, you're pretty smart for a twelve year old."

A little girl goes up to her mom and asks, "What's that?" And the mom answers, "A vagina." Then the little girl asks, "Well, when am I gonna get one?" And the mom answers, "As soon as you grow up."

Then the little girl goes up to her dad and asks, "What's that?" And the dad answers, "A penis." So the little girl asks, "Well, when am I gonna get one?" And the dad answers, "As soon as your mom goes to work."

A man's wife had been in a coma for several days following a particularly nasty knock on the head. As usual, one of the nurses in the hospital was giving her a wash in bed. As she washed down the woman's body, she sponged her pubic hair. Out of the corner of her eye she thought she saw the woman's eyebrows shudder. Not quite sure, she tried again. This time, she actually did see some movement.

"Doctor, Doctor," she called, "I saw some movement!"

The doctor came into the room and tried as well. Once more, they both saw movement around the woman's eyes.

"Well, this is good news," said the doctor. "I think we should call her husband and let him know."

So they called her husband and told him that they had seen some movement. When he arrived, they explained that by touching her pubic hair they were seeing some sort of reaction in her facial muscles. The doctor suggested that the husband might like to try something a little more adventurous in order to provoke a stronger reaction.

"I suggest that we leave the room and that you try a little oral sex," he said.

The husband duly agreed and so he was left alone in the room. Several moments later, all the emergency alarms and buzzers were activated. The doctor and a host of nurses ran into the wife's room, where they saw the husband zipping up his jeans.

"Oops," he said, "I think I choked her."

One Friday afternoon two women are sitting on the front porch.

The first woman says, "Here comes my husband with a bunch of flowers. That means I'll be on my back with my legs in the air all weekend."

The other woman asks, "Why? Don't you have a vase?"

A mangy redneck youth walks into the kitchen, where his mom is fixing that night's dinner.

"Mom, I got a splinter in my finger. Can I have a glass of cider?" asks the slack-jawed youth.

"Are you sure you don't want me to pull it out?"

"No, thanks. Just the cider."

"Well, sure," responds the youth's mother, and she gives her boy the cider and watches him trot contentedly off.

About fifteen minutes later the boy returns to

the kitchen and again asks his mother for a glass of cider. His mother, not wanting to question his reasoning, gives him another glass and again watches him leave happy.

Ten minutes later the boy returns once again and asks for a glass of cider.

The mother complies with her son's wishes again, but her curiosity has been piqued to the point where she can't resist knowing why any longer. So she wanders into the family room and sees her son sitting in front of the TV with his finger in the glass.

"Why on earth do you have your finger in that glass?" asks the boy's mother.

"Well, Mom, I heard sis on the phone say that, whenever she had a prick in her hand, she couldn't wait to get it in cider."

SEX AND ROADKILL

What do you get when you cross a car and a dog?
A carpet.

_____

How do you make a cat go woof?
Douse it in gas, strike a match, and then voilá: *whoof!*

_____

Why do dogs lick their dicks?
Because they can't make a fist.

How do you make a cat drink?
Put it in the blender and extract the fur.

———————

What has two legs and bleeds?
Half a dog.

———————

A bear and a rabbit are both taking a dump in the woods. The bear turns to the rabbit and asks, "Do you have a problem with poop sticking to your fur?"

The rabbit replies, "Why, no. Never."

At that, the bear grabs the rabbit and wipes his butt.

———————

Two whales were swimming along, looking for fish to eat, but the waters were empty due to a boat that was catching all the fish. The boy whale said to his companion, "I have a plan. Let's swim up underneath the boat, and when we're right underneath, we'll blow our spouts as hard as we can. That'll knock the boat over, and then we'll eat everything and everyone that falls into the water.''

The girl whale thought for a moment, then shook her head. "I don't mind the blow job," she said. "But I draw the line at swallowing seamen!"

What is green, slimy, and smells like pork?
  Kermit the Frog's dick.

What do you do if you come across an elephant in the jungle?
  Wipe it off and say you're sorry.

This guy sits down at a restaurant, and when the waiter comes over to see if he has any questions, the guy puts down the menu and says, "How do you prepare your chickens?"

"Well, sir, there's not much to it. We just flat out tell them they're going to die."

———————

A certain zoo had acquired a very rare species of gorilla. Within a few weeks the gorilla, a female, became very ornery and difficult to handle. Upon examination, the zoo veterinarian determined the problem: She was in heat. What to do? There was no male of this species available.

While reflecting on their problem, the zoo administrators noticed Mike, an employee responsible for cleaning the animals' cages. Now Mike, it was rumored, possessed ample ability to satisfy any female, and he wasn't very bright. So the zoo administrators thought they might have a solution. Perhaps they could entice Mike to satisfy the female gorilla. So he was approached with a proposition: Would he be willing to screw the gorilla—for five hundred bucks? Mike replied that he might be interested, but he would have to think the matter over.

The following day, Mike announced that he would accept their offer, but only under three conditions. "First," he said, "I don't want to have to kiss her. Second, I want nothing to do with any offspring that may result from this union."

The zoo administrator quickly agreed to these conditions, but what could be the third?

"Well," said Mike, "You've gotta give me another week to come up with the five hundred bucks."

———————

What is red and green and goes two hundred MPH?

A frog in a blender.

———————

One day, while an elephant was walking through the woods, she got a thorn stuck in her foot. She saw an ant passing and asked him to help her get the thorn out.

The ant asked, "What do I get in return?"

The elephant replied, "If you get it out, I'll have sex with you."

So the ant gets busy taking the thorn out. When he finally gets it out, he looks up at the elephant and says, "Okay, it's out. Are you ready?"

The elephant thinks, *Hey, what's a little ant gonna do anyway?*

The ant climbs up and starts to work away.

Just then a monkey overhead drops a coconut on the elephant's head.

"Ouch," screams the elephant, and the ant responds, "Yeah, take it all bitch."

———————

A lion is drinking from a puddle and his tail is up. A gorilla walks up behind him, seizes the opportunity, and slips the lion a Liberace.

The gorilla takes off, and the lion takes off after him. The gorilla runs into a hunter's camp, jumps into a tent, puts on a safari outfit, grabs a copy of the *Johannesburg Times,* sits down, and starts to read. The lion runs into the camp, sticks his head into the tent, and roars, "Arrgg! Did a gorilla come through here?"

The gorilla says, "You mean the one that fucked the lion in the ass?"

The lion says, "My, God! You mean it's in the paper already?"

An Aussie was marooned on a desert island. His only companions were a male dog and a female koala. The dog and koala hit it off, and for a year, the Aussie could only sit and watch while the dog humped the koala senseless.

Lucky bastard! thought the Aussie. *I could do with a good shag myself.*

One day a beautiful naked blonde was washed up on the beach.

"Hi. I'll do anything you want me to," she said to the Aussie.

"Great! At last, after all this time! Take the dog for a walk, love, while I shag this koala."

———————

A man was driving down a quiet country lane when out onto the road strayed a rooster. *Whack!* The rooster disappeared under the car in a cloud of feathers. Shaken, the man pulled over at a nearby farmhouse and rang the doorbell. A farmer appeared. The man somewhat nervously said, "I think I killed your rooster. Please allow me to replace him."

"Suit yourself," the farmer replied. "The hens are round the back."

Two guys are walking down the street and see a dog on the lawn licking his balls.

One guy says to the other, "Man, I sure wish I could do that."

The other guy says, "Don't you think you ought to pet him first?"

A man was feeling very depressed. So he walked into a bar and ordered a triple scotch.

As the bartender poured him the drink, he remarked, "That's quite a heavy drink. What's wrong?"

After quickly downing his drink, the man replied, "I got home and found my wife having sex with my best friend."

"Wow!" exclaimed the bartender as he poured the man a second triple scotch. "No wonder you needed a stiff drink. The second triple is on the house."

As the man downed his second triple scotch, the bartender asked him, "What did you do?"

The man replied, "I walked over to him, looked him right in the eye and said, 'Bad dog!' "

An elderly Scot is sitting in a bar talking to the bartender.

"Lad, look out there at the field. Do you see that fence? Look how well it's built. I built that fence stone by stone with my own two hands. Piled it for months. But do they call me McGregor, the fence builder? No."

Then the old man gestured at the bar.

"Look here at the bar. Do you see how smooth and just it is? I planed that surface down myself. I carved that wood with my own hard labor for eight days. But do they call me McGregor, the bar builder? No."

Then the old man looks around nervously, trying to make sure no one is paying attention.

"But you fuck one goat . . ."

This woman is driving into a small town, and she slams on the brakes as a coyote runs across the road in front of her. Just as she regains her wits and gets ready to proceed, a cowboy runs right in front of her and catches the coyote by the hind legs and starts screwing it.

"Oh, my God!" she exclaims and drives into town to find the local law. She sees the sheriff's car parked in front of the town bar. "It figures," she says as she storms inside. The first thing she notices is an old, old man with a long white beard sitting in the corner jacking off. She runs up to the sheriff, who's sitting at the bar with his drink.

"What kind of sick town are you running here? I drive into town and almost run over some cowboy sodomizing an animal. And then I come in here and see this old man in the corner jacking off in public!"

"Well, madam," the sheriff slowly replies, "you don't expect him to catch a coyote at his age, do you?"

———————

A researcher is conducting a survey into sheep fucking. First of all he visits an Iowa farmer.

"So, Iowa farmer, how do you ball your sheep?"

"Well, I take the hind legs of the sheep and put them down my rubber boots and take the front legs of the sheep and put them over a fence."

"That's very interesting," replies the researcher and he leaves the Iowa farmer. Then he meets a Kansas farmer.

"So, Kansas farmer, how do you do your sheep?"

"Well, I take the hind legs of the sheep and put them down my rubber boots and take the front legs of the sheep and put them over a fence."

"That's very interesting," replies the researcher. "That's how they do it in Iowa too." And he leaves the Kansas farmer. Then he meets a farmer from Arkansas.

"So, Arkansas farmer, how do you screw your sheep?"

"Well, I take the hind legs of the sheep and put them down my rubber boots and take the front legs of the sheep and put them over my shoulders."

"Over your shoulders?" replies the researcher. "Don't you put them over a fence like everyone else?"

"What?" says the farmer. "And miss out on all the kissing?"

A pit bull, a bulldog, and a black lab are all locked up in the local dog pound. The pit bull decides to speak freely and says, "You know, it wasn't my fault I bit that kid's head off. Those kids have been throwing rocks at me for years and I just couldn't help but jump the fence one day and go after them. Now they're going to put me to sleep."

The bulldog speaks up and says, "I'm in for a similar incident. My master just wasn't paying any attention to me since that stinkin' baby came along and one day while it was crawlin' around on the floor I bit its leg off. Now they are going to put me to sleep too."

Both the pit bull and bulldog look at the black lab and ask, "What are you in for?"

The lab replies, "Well, the other day my master's lady was walking around the house naked all day long cleaning the house. When she went into the bathroom and bent over to clean the tub I just couldn't take it anymore. I came up behind her, put my front paws on her back, and fucked her."

The pit bull asks, "So when are you due to be put to sleep?"

And the lab replies, "Shit, I'm just in to have my nails trimmed."

A schoolteacher announced to her third grade class that the subject for the day was farm animals.

"Can anyone tell me what sound a chicken makes?" she asked.

"Cluck, cluck, cluck," Billy answered proudly.

"That's correct, Billy," the teacher said. "Does anyone know what a cow says?"

Jenny's hand shot up as she yelled, "Mooooooo!"

"Good, Jenny. Now who knows what a pig sounds like?" she asked.

From the back of the class, little Paul shouted, "Freeze, Mutherfucker!"

EAT YOUR HEART OUT

What did the cannibal do after he dumped his girlfriend?

Wiped his ass.

———————

What's the definition of "trust?"

Two cannibals giving each other a blow job.

———————

Two cannibals, a father and a son, were elected by the tribe to go out and hunt for something to eat. They walked deep into the jungle and waited by a path. Before long, along came this little old man.

The son said, "Oh, Dad, there's one."

"No," said the father. "There's not enough

meat on that one to feed the dogs. We'll just wait."

Well, a little while later, along came this really overweight man.

The son said, "Hey, Dad, he's plenty big enough."

"No," said the father. "We'll all die of a heart attack from the fat in that one. We'll just wait."

About an hour later, this absolutely gorgeous woman walks by.

The son said, "Now there's nothing wrong with that one, Dad. Let's eat her."

"No," said the father. "We will not eat her either."

"Why not?" asked the son.

"We're going to take her back alive and eat your mother!"

————————

A native comes out of the jungle to his wife with a python in one hand and a small tribesman in the other. Just as he's getting to his wife, she shouts out, "Oh, no, not snake-and-pygmy pie again!"

Why don't cannibals eat clowns?
  They taste funny.

———————

Jeffrey Dahmer had his mother over for dinner when she suddenly said, "You know, Jeffrey, I don't like your neighbors."
  "Then just eat the vegetables."

PRIVATE PARTS

What is the difference between your wages and your penis?

You can always find a girl to blow your wages!

What's the difference between a good blow job and your wife?

About fifty dollars.

A lady walks into a hardware store to buy a hinge. The guy behind the counter says, "Do you wanna screw for that hinge?"

"No, but I'll blow you for a toaster!"

A good friend is someone who goes downtown to get two blow jobs and comes back and gives you one.

_____

How do you know who gives good blow jobs?
  Word of mouth!

_____

What's so great about an Ethiopian blow job?
  You know she'll swallow.

_____

What is hard and hairy on the outside, soft and wet on the inside, begins with the letter "c" ends with the letter "t" and has the letters "u" and "n" in the middle?
  A coconut.

Girl to the dentist: I'd rather have a baby than have a tooth pulled out.

Dentist: Make up your mind so I know which tool to use.

———————

What's better than honor?
   In 'er!

———————

Two housewives met in the local supermarket. One had filled her shopping trolley with Vaseline. She explained, "They're going to raise the price soon, so I'm stocking up."

The other woman replied, "I'd never go to such extremes to save money. I'm not that tight."

A hot young couple is getting it on in the backseat of a car. Things are really getting steamy when the girl finally gasps, "Baby, kiss me where it smells."

"Whatever it takes," the guy says and drives her to New Jersey.

_____

What do you get if you cross a penis and a potato?
   A dictator.

_____

What's pink and hard and drips when it gets pumped up?
   A weightlifting pig!

_____

This woman stands up on a bar stool and yells, "I don't fuck anybody unless he's got a twelve-inch cock!

This guy in the corner yells out, "I don't cut off two inches for anybody!"

A ninety-year-old man goes to a hooker. When he gets undressed, she looks at his limp dick and says "Mister, you've had it!"

"Thank you very much," he says. "How much do I owe you?"

———————

Two little boys are talking in the backyard.

"My daddy's got a penis," says the first.

"My daddy's got two penises," says the second.

"No way," says the first.

"Yeah," says the second. "He's got a small one to pee with and a great big one to clean the baby-sitter's teeth!

———————

A woman asks a Scotsman what is up his kilt.

"Why don't you put your hand up and find out?" he says.

"It's gruesome!" she shouts.

"Put your hand up again and it'll grue some more!"

"Adam came first," said the minister from the pulpit.

"But men always do," shouted the ladies in the congregation

A woman was walking down the street one day with her left breast hanging out. An elderly gent noticing this and did the honorable thing. He approached the woman saying, "Excuse me, madam, but your left breast is protruding."

"Jesus Christ," came the reply. "I've left the baby on the bus."

Did you hear about the girl who had a glass plate put in her stomach?

She had a womb with a view.

There's an old man sitting on his porch rocking in his rocking chair, and a little boy walks by carrying some chicken wire.

The old man says "Boy! Where you goin' with that chicken wire?"

The boy answers, "I'm gonna catch me some chickens."

The old man says, "Boy, you can't catch chickens with chicken wire."

The kid just walks past and the old man shakes his head. About an hour later the kid comes back with dozens of chickens. The next day the old man is rocking on his porch, and the same boy walks by with some duct tape. The old man says "Boy! Where you goin' with that duct tape?"

The kid says, "I'm gonna catch me some ducks."

The man says, "Boy, you can't catch ducks with duct tape."

The kid walks by and the old man just shakes his head. About an ·hour later the kid comes back with dozens of ducks.

The next day the old man is rocking on his porch, and the boy walks by with a pussy willow branch. The old man says "Boy! Wait right there. I'm gonna get my coat!"

What do lobster thermidor and oral sex have in common?

You can't get either of them at home.

What are the two biggest lies in Poland?

"The check is in your mouth."

"I won't come in the mail."

What do you call "6.9?"

A good 69 interrupted by a period.

What do you call a "period?"

A bloody waste of fucking time.

Why do women have periods?
  Because they deserve them.

_____

How did the Puerto Rican woman know that her daughter was having her period?
  She could taste the blood on her son's dick.

_____

Why do men have assholes?
  So they won't be total pricks.

_____

This Pole got married, but he was too dumb to know what to do on his wedding night.
  "For God's sake, Stan," said his bride, "you take that thing you play with and you put it where I pee."
  So he got up and threw his bowling ball in the sink.

Your basic virgin female was all set to get married to a virile Greek when her mother took her aside for a little prenuptial advice.

"Dear, I know you love this man," the mother began. "And we've tried to welcome him into our family. But there is something you must know. These Greeks like to make love in a disgusting way, so if he ever asks you to turn over before making love, *don't* do it. It's degrading and painful, and it will ruin your marriage."

So the wedding is fine. The happy couple enjoys their first month of marital bliss until one night the Greek says to his wife, "Honey, let's try making love a little differently tonight. Why don't you roll over?"

The woman loses it. "You brute," she sobs. "My mother warned me about you. I can't believe you would do this to me."

"But, honey," the startled Greek replies, "I just thought you might want to have children."

GROSS LEPER AND BABY JOKES

Did you hear about the leper playing poker?
He threw in a rotten hand.

———————

What's the definition of a "skeleton?"
A leper in a wind tunnel.

———————

Why did the leper fail his driving test?
He left his foot on the gas.

What's red and sits in a tree?
   Sanitary Owl.

_____

What's black, bangs on the window, and screams?
   A baby in a microwave.

_____

What goes: *Plop! Plop! Fizz!*
   Two babies in an acid bath.

_____

What do they call a leper in a hot tub?
   Stu.

How do you make a dead baby float?
    A scoop of ice cream and a scoop of dead baby.

––––––––––

Why did they call off the hockey game at the leper colony?
    There was a face off in the corner.

––––––––––

How do you get a leper out of bed?
    With a shovel.

––––––––––

What did the leper say to the prostitute?
    Keep the tip.

Why did the leper get thrown out of the party?
    The guests kept mistaking his neck for the cheese dip.

———————

What is red and silver and crawls into walls?
    A baby with forks in its eyes.

———————

What do you call a leper in a swimming pool?
    String cheese.

GROSS GOLF
JOKES

A man goes golfing with his friend Harry. He arrives home several hours late. His wife asks, "What took you so long?"

He replies, "Oh, Ethel, it was a horrible afternoon! On the third hole, Harry had a heart attack and died on the spot!"

Ethel says, "Oh, darling! It must have been awful for you!"

The husband replies, "It was hell! Fifteen holes of 'hit the ball, drag Harry, hit the ball, drag Harry . . .'"

A couple of women were playing golf one sunny Saturday morning. The first of the two-some teed off and watched in horror as her ball headed directly toward a foursome of men playing the next hole. Indeed, the ball hit one of the men, and he immediately clasped his hands together at his crotch, fell to the ground, and proceeded to roll around in evident agony.

The woman rushed down to the man and immediately began to apologize. She explained that she was a physical therapist. "Please allow me to help. I'm a physical therapist and I know I could relieve your pain if you'd just allow me!"

"I'll be all right. I'll be fine in a few minutes," he replied breathlessly as he remained in the fetal position still clasping his hands together at his crotch.

But she persisted, and he finally allowed her to help him. She gently took his hands away and laid them to the side, she loosened his pants, and she put her hands inside. She began to massage his crotch. She then asked him, "How does that feel?"

"It feels great, but my thumb still hurts like hell!"

What's the difference between a G-spot and a golf ball?

A man will spend twenty minutes looking for a golf ball.

What is the difference between looking for a lost golf ball and Lady Godiva?

The former is a hunt on the course . . .

LESBIAN AND
GAY JOKES

What does a gay call a used condom?
  Seal-a-Meal

———————

Why was the gay expelled from the leper colony?
  Some bum split on him.

———————

What's the difference between a gay and a micro-wave?
  You don't get your meat brown in a microwave.

What does a lonely gay guy do when he is horny?
   He shits in his hand, then jerks off.

_____

What did one gay coroner say to the other gay coroner?
   "Whaddya say we run out back and suck down a cold one?"

_____

What's the most popular pick up line in a gay bar?
   "May I push in your stool?"

_____

What did one lesbian frog say to the other?
   "Gee, we really do taste like chicken."

What's the difference between a refrigerator and a gay guy?

The refrigerator doesn't say, "Ohhh" when you pull the meat out.

———————

Michael Jackson and his wife are in the recovery room with their new baby son. The doctor walks in and Michael asks, "Doctor, how long before we can have sex?"

The doctor replies, "I'd wait until he's at least fourteen."

———————

A guy is in a bus station, and he goes into the men's room to piss. When he walks in, he see a leprechaun with an enormous dick. As he pees, he cannot avoid spying on the giant member of the tiny man dressed in green.

The leprechaun zips up and the man asks him if he is indeed a real leprechaun. The little man says, "Aye, me boy, I'm a leprechaun, and I can grant you three wishes."

"Oh, neat," comes the reply, "What do I need to do?"

"Well, havin' such a large cock makes it a bit

awkward with the ladies, the thing not fittin'
and all. I'll grant you your three wishes if you
wouldn't mind suckin' me dick until I come."

The man is a bit taken aback, but agrees
because he knows he can wish for anything he
wants later. After the green man has come, he
starts to walk away.

The guy says, "Hey, what about my three
wishes?"

The leprechaun asks, "How old are you me
boy?"

"Twenty-five," he says.

"Aren't you a bit too old to still be believin'
in leprechauns?"

———————

Why do you have to wrap duct tape around a
gerbil?

So that it doesn't explode when you sodomize
it.

———————

What did one lesbian vampire say to the other
lesbian vampire?

"See you next month!"

Why do Japanese Sumo wrestlers shave their legs?

So you can tell them apart from radical lesbian feminists.

———————

This plumber was working hard to clear up a stuffed toilet in a San Francisco bar. The bowl was literally overflowing with shit and he wasn't keeping up. Suddenly three gay guys walk in and one starts screaming excitedly while the other two reach for their wallets.

"See, see," the faggot screamed, "who says there's no such thing as a free lunch."

———————

A gay walks into a bar, walks up to one guy, and says "I'll give you twenty bucks if you let me screw you up the butt!"

The guy cringes and says "Frigging homo! Get out of my face!"

The gay goes to the next guy and offers the same thing.

The guy says "Man, go away. You make me sick."

The gay comes to a wino at the end of the bar and offers the same thing.

The wino says "Well, okay," and he stumbles out the back door. The gay proceeds to screw the wino up the butt when all of a sudden the wino shits all over the gay guy. I mean, the stuff is running everywhere.

The gay jumps back and says, "Shit, man! What the hell did you do that for?"

The wino says innocently "What? I cum too soon?"

———————

What do you call two lesbians on their period?

Fingerpainting.

TOTALLY GROSS ONE LINERS

How can you tell if an Arkansas girl is old enough to marry?

Make her stand in a barrel. If her chin is over the top, she's old enough. If it isn't, cut the barrel down a bit.

How do you embarrass an archaeologist?

Give him a used tampon and ask him which period it came from.

How can you tell if your wife is dead?
   The sex is the same but the dishes pile up.

———————————

Why are men like laxatives?
   They irritate the shit out of you.

———————————

What do a gynecologist and a Domino's delivery man have in common?
   They both get to smell the pie but neither one of them can eat it.

———————————

Why does Dr. Pepper come in a bottle?
   His wife died.

How can you tell if you've got a bulimic stripper at a batchelor party?

The cake jumps out of the girl.

How do you recycle toilet paper?

Hang it on the wall and bash the shit out of it.

What do you call a prostitute with a runny nose?

Full.

What's the difference between strange pussy and apple pie?

You can eat your Mom's apple pie without being afraid.

Why do Southern guys go to family reunions?
  To meet chicks.

———————

What do a bleached blonde and a 747 have in common?
  They both have little black boxes.

———————

What is the difference between tampons and mobile phones?
  Mobile phones are for assholes.

———————

How do you get a dog to stop humping your leg?
  Pick him up and start sucking his dick.

What's the difference between a downhill putt and a blow job?

You'll never hear a guy getting a blow job say, "Slow down. Stop. *Bite, you cocksucker!*"

—————————

How do you make five pounds of fat look good?
Put a nipple on it.

—————————

What's the difference between oral sex and anal sex?

Oral sex makes your day. Anal sex makes your *whole* week.

—————————

The Answer: A cock robin.
The Question: What are you putting in my mouth, Batman?

Why are women like Kentucky Fried Chicken?
Once you're finished with the breasts and the thighs, all you are left with is a greasy box!

_____

How is pubic hair like parsley?
You push it to the side before you start eating.

_____

Why don't blondes water-ski?
Because they lie down as soon as their crotches get wet.

_____

What do you call the inanimate tissue around a vagina?
A woman.

_____

What do you call a vegetarian with diarrhea?
A salad shooter

What is the difference between women and computers?

A women will not take a 3.25-inch floppy.

———————

If your wife keeps coming out of the kitchen to nag at you, what have you done wrong?

Made her chain too long.

———————

What do a tornado, a hurricane, and a redneck divorce have in common?

Somebody's fixin' to lose a trailer home.

———————

What's the difference between a blonde and a mosquito?

If you slap a mosquito, it'll stop sucking.

———————

Why don't Baptists make love standing up?

Because it might lead to dancing.

What's the difference between love, true love, and showing off?
Spit, swallow, and gargle.

———————

What's the difference between E.T. and a man?
E.T. phoned home.

———————

What has four legs and eight arms?
A pit bull terrier at a children's play area.

———————

Why do cavemen drag their women by the hair?
Because if they dragged them by the feet, they would fill up with mud.

If you see a lawyer on a bicycle, why don't you swerve to hit him?

It might be your bicycle.

———————————

Did you hear about the new blonde paint?

It's not real bright, but it's cheap and spreads easy.

———————————

What's the difference between the Rolling Stones and a Scotsman?

One says "Hey, you, get off of my cloud." The other says, "Hey, McCloud, get off of my ewe."

———————————

How do men sort their laundry?

"Filthy" and "Filthy but wearable."

What are two reasons why men don't mind their own business?
1. No mind.
2. No business.

———————

What's the difference between acne and a priest?
Acne usually comes on a boy's face *after* he turns thirteen.

———————

What have men and floor tiles got in common?
If you lay them properly, you can walk on them for the rest of your life!

———————

What do you call a woman who just lost ninety-five percent of her intelligence?
Single!

———————

What's the fastest way to get a nun pregnant?
Dress her up as an altar boy.

What do you call a bleached blonde standing on her head?

A brunette with bad breath!

What's the difference between driving in the fog and eating pussy?

At least when you are eating pussy you can see the asshole in front of you.

How are men and parking spaces a lot alike?

The good ones are always taken and the rest are handicapped.

Why is a Laundromat a bad place for a guy to pick up women?

Because a woman who can't even afford a washing machine will never be able to support you.

Why is a necrophiliac like a grave digger?
    They both dig dead people's holes.

———————

How do you know if a guy has a high sperm count?
    His girlfriend has to chew before swallowing!

———————

Why can't you tell blondes knock-knock jokes?
    Because they go and answer the fucking door.

———————

How many women does it take to paint a wall?
    Depends on how hard you throw them.

———————

Why is a "Pap smear" called a "Pap smear?"
    Because women wouldn't do them if they were called "cunt scrapes."

What do an anniversary and a toilet have in common?
  Men always miss them.

———————

Why do they call it PMS?
  Because Mad Cow Disease came too late.

———————

Why don't women blink during foreplay?
  They don't have time.

———————

What do you call a truck driver with a load of sheep headed for Montana?
  A pimp.

———————

Why do women have two sets of lips?
  So they can piss and moan at the same time.

What do you call a redneck who doesn't fuck his sister?

An only child.

––––––––––––

What happens if a woman puts her panties on backward?

She gets her ass chewed out.

––––––––––––

What goes: "*Click*—is that it? *Click*—is that it? *Click*—is that it?"

A blind person with a Rubic's cube.

––––––––––––

Did you hear about the new morning-after pill for men?

If changes their blood type.

––––––––––––

What do you call a Florida gynecologist?

A spreader of old wives' tails.

How do you know when a blonde is having a bad day?

She can't find her pencil and her tampon is behind her ear!

———————

Why did God create woman?

To carry semen from the bedroom to the toilet.

———————

Why are men like spray paint?

One squeeze and they're all over you.

———————

Why is cream more expensive that milk?

Because cows find it harder to sit on the smaller bottles.

———————

Why did the gynecologist use two fingers?

He wanted a second opinion.

What's the difference between a mugger and a peeping tom?

A mugger snatches watches.

———————

What's the definition of a "virgin?"

An ugly third grader.

———————

What's black and blue and hates sex?

A rape victim.

———————

What do you do when you're finished fucking a ten-year-old girl?

Turn her over and pretend she's a ten-year-old boy!

———————

How do you circumcise a redneck?

Kick his sister in the chin.

What's eighteen inches long and makes women scream all night?
Crib death.

_____

What does a girl with bulimia call two fingers?
Dessert.

_____

Why did the blonde stare at orange juice for two hours?
Because it said concentrate!

_____

Why did Humpty Dumpty push his girlfriend off the wall?
So he could see her crack!

Why did God make piss yellow and cum white?
    So the Irish would know whether they were coming or going.

———————

When do you slap a midget?
    When he tells your wife her hair smells nice.

———————

Why didn't the blonde go to the movies on buck night?
    Because she couldn't fit the deer into her car.

———————

What do you call a blonde with two brain cells?
    Pregnant.

DISGUSTING
LISTS

GETTING OFF ON "GASMS"

Sex in a boat—oar-gasms.
Sex with a nerd—dork-gasms.
Sex at the entrance to your house—door-gasms.
Sex on carpet or linoleum—floor-gasms.
Sex at the supermarket—store-gasms.
Sex at a Steven King movie—horror-gasms.
Sex with a prostitute—whore-gasms.
Sex with an accountant—bore-gasms.
Sex with stuffed donkeys—Eyeore-gasms.
Sex while broke—poor-gasms.
Sex with a lion—roar-gasms.
Sex for hours and hours on end—sore-gasms.
Sex on a golf course—fore-gasms.
Sex with a nymphomaniac—more-gasms.
Sex with a dermatologist—pore-gasms.
Sex with a politician—Al Gore-gasms.
Sex with chocolate, marshmallows, and graham crackers—s'more-gasms.
Sex with a bullfighter—toreador-gasms.
Sex on the beach—shore-gasms.
Sex in Asia—Singapore-gasms.

Sex in the vicinity of a garbage can—odor-gasms.

Sex on the way to the train—"All Aboard"-gasms.

Sex that wasn't very satisfying—"There's the door"-gasms.

Sex with someone who's not paying attention—ignore-gasms.

Sex with a competitive partner—score-gasms.

Sex while flying—soar-gasms.

Sex with a meat-eater—carnivore-gasms.

Sex with a person who's got a really bad hairdo—pompadore-gasms.

Sex with a big dog—labrador-gasms.

Sex with Bevis and Butthead—"Gonna Score"-gasms.

Sex with three of your friends—four-gasms.

Sex with a Norse god—Thor-gasms.

———————

32 REASONS WHY COOKIE DOUGH IS BETTER THAN MEN

1. It's enjoyable hard or soft.

2. It makes a mess too, but it tastes better.

3. It doesn't mind if you take your anger out on it.

4. You always want to swallow.

5. It won't complain if you share it with friends.

6. It's quick and convenient.

7. You can enjoy it more than once.

8. It comes already protectively wrapped.

9. You can make it as large as you want.

10. If you don't finish it you can save it for later.

11. It's easier to get the kind you want.

12. You can comparison shop.

13. It's easier to find in a grocery store.

14. You can put it away when you've had enough.

15. You know yours has never been eaten before.

16. It won't complain if you chew on it.

17. It comes chocolate flavored.

18. You always know when to get rid of it.

19. You can return it—satisfaction is guaranteed.

20. It's always ready to go.

21. You won't get arrested if you eat it in public.

22. You don't have to change the sheets if you eat it in bed.

23. It won't wake you up because it's hard.

24. You don't have to find an excuse not to eat it.

25. You can tell your friends how much you've eaten without sounding like you're bragging.

26. It won't take up room in your bed.

27. It's easy to pick up.

28. You never have unwanted cookie dough chasing you around.

29. You know what the extra weight is from.

30. It won't get jealous if you pick up another one.

31. It never has an insecurity problem with its size.

32. It is very pliable.

Get Grossed Out
With More Jokes by Julius Alvin

__Awesomely Gross Jokes	0-8217-3613-2	$3.50US/$4.50CAN
__Agonizingly Gross Jokes	0-8217-3648-5	$3.50US/$4.50CAN
__Brutally Gross Jokes	0-8217-5884-5	$4.99US/$6.50CAN
__Intensely Gross Jokes	0-8217-4168-3	$3.50US/$4.50CAN
__Insanely Gross Jokes	0-8217-5682-6	$4.99US/$6.50CAN
__Obnoxiously Gross Jokes	0-8217-6177-3	$4.99US/$6.50CAN
__Outrageously Gross Jokes	0-8217-5784-9	$4.99US/$6.50CAN
__Unbelievably Gross Jokes	0-8217-5950-7	$4.99US/$6.50CAN
__Wildly Gross Jokes	0-8217-5350-9	$4.99US/$5.99CAN
__Best of Gross Jokes I	0-8217-5469-6	$4.99US/$6.50CAN
__Best of Gross Jokes II	0-8217-5602-8	$4.99US/$6.50CAN
__The Big Book of Gross Jokes	1-57566-235-3	$8.00US/$13.00CAN
__The Bigger Book of Gross Jokes	1-57566-362-7	$9.00US/$14.00CAN

Call toll free **1-888-345-BOOK** to order by phone or use this coupon to order by mail.
Name_____
Address_____
City _____ State _____Zip_____
Please send me the books I have checked above.
I am enclosing $_____
Plus postage and handling* $_____
Sales tax (in New York and Tennessee) $_____
Total amount enclosed $_____
*Add $2.50 for the first book and $.50 for each additional book.
Send check or money order (no cash or CODs) to:
Kensington Publishing Corp., 850 Third Avenue, New York, NY 10022
Prices and Numbers subject to change without notice.
All orders subject to availability.
Check out our website at **www.kensingtonbooks.com**